Ten Things Should

about Reading, Writing and Math:

4th Grade

MW01115251

by

Danita Smith

Copyright © 2016 Danita Smith

Red and Black Ink, LLC

ISBN: 0-9971386-0-2

ISBN-13: 978-0-9971386-0-3

DEDICATION

This book is dedicated to our future
and our children.

by Danita Smith

Table of Contents

Intro.	Brief Overview	Pg. 1
Ch. 1	Fourth Grade	Pg. 5
Ch. 2	Fourth-Grade Math	Pg. 9
Ch. 3	Fourth-Grade Mathematical Skills	Pg. 19
Ch. 4	Mathematical Activities	Pg. 23
Ch. 5	Reading and Writing in Fourth Grade	Pg. 33
Ch. 6	Fourth-Grade Reading and Writing Skills	Pg. 49
Ch. 7	Reading and Writing Activites	Pg. 53
Ch. 8	Parent/Teacher Conferences	Pg. 63
Ch. 9	Education Success Stories: Thurgood Marshall	Pg. 71

by Danita Smith

Introduction

This book offers a simple approach toward helping you oversee and evaluate your child's educational development in three key areas: reading, writing, and mathematics. These three areas are the foundation for educational success at any grade level. Thus, this book highlights **selected** skills and knowledge.

There is no way to determine if each school across the country will teach the exact same skills, at the exact same time, and during the exact same grades (which is one of the reasons why I wrote this book); however, this book gives you an idea of what might be taught at this given grade level and an idea of skills you can make sure your child is developing. The skills listed in this book were compiled as a result of research on recommendations for national educational standards, various state guidelines, and largely personal experience.[1234]

They are a selection of skills that you can look at in order to help you evaluate and manage your child's educational progress in key areas. Therefore the areas and activities outlined in this book are designed to help you in several ways:

1. To help you to proactively manage your child's education by giving you an idea of selected skills your child might be taught in this grade.

2. To provide you with a list of activities that you can use to supplement your child's education at home.

3. To help you identify areas where your child may need additional instruction, even before a teacher points them out to you.

There are five key principles highlighted in this book that may help you approach your child's educational development.

---

[1] National Council of Teachers of Mathematics. http://www.nctm.org/

[2] Online Oregon Standards Newspaper, Oregon Department of Education. http://www.ode.state.or.us/teachlearn/real/newspaper/default.aspx

[3] Educational Standards, Education World U.S. http://www.education-world.com/standards/national/index.shtml

[4] National Council of Teachers of English. http://www.ncte.org/about/over/standards

1. **Parental (Adult) Involvement:** Be involved in your child's education.

2. **Educational Exposure At Home:** Expose your child to educational concepts at home.

3. **Repetition and Practice:** Develop and reinforce your child's skills through repetition and practice.

4. **Encouraged Articulation:** Instruct your child to articulate his or her views in writing and verbally.

5. **Positive Reinforcement:** Encourage and reward your child when he or she displays the behaviors you are looking for when it comes to learning and school (HAVE FUN!).

Chapter 1
Fourth Grade

Your youngster is now in the fourth grade and the transformation that has taken place since kindergarten may be amazing to you. Your child came into school knowing little about how to read and write; little about addition and subtraction. Now, she is able to read complete books on her own, she can write in complete sentences, and she not only knows how to add and subtract, she can multiply as well.

You can really see her independence as a learner begin to take shape. But now is not the time to let go of the reins; she still needs your support and guidance. You will really begin to see new information come to life for your child in is grade. Since she has much of the foundational skills :eded for school, she will be exposed to many more new concepts and ideas. She will be asked to process new information and to understand the basic knowledge upon which many of our subjects are based.

For instance, in social studies she may start to learn more about how our country is structured. She may learn all of the fifty states and their capitals along with the idea of what a state is vs. a city. She may also be introduced to basic concepts in science like mass, density, and matter.

More information and techniques will be taught to her about how to do a research paper. She may be given the basics about how to go to different sources for information. Information can be obtained from books, from the Internet, from magazines, etc. Many of the projects she will work on will be conducted to teach her "how" to go about doing such research projects so that in later years she will have the skills needed to complete any project that is asked of her.

She will develop additional skills in mathematics, including advancing with division, handling fractions and decimals, and multiplying numbers with multiple digits. The lessons she has learned in earlier grades will really pay off here.

This may also be the first time she will receive "letter" grades as a part of her report card and on tests and quizzes. This can be a little bit of a change for some children, but it gives them a clear understanding of where they stand relative to mastering the material, based on the teacher's assessment. Remember, it is really important that you do not rely on grades alone to assess your child's development. While grades can be an accurate assessment of your child's understanding of a given subject as presented in a given class, they may not always be an accurate assessment of your child's understanding of that subject overall.

I remember having a conversation with a high school student who was taking a U.S. government class. She was studying the Declaration of Independence in class and was working on an assignment related to it. She wanted some help with the assignment, so I asked her a couple of questions to get her started, such as, "What country did the American Colonies go to war with during the Revolutionary War and why?"

She knew who was involved in the war, but had trouble explaining why we went to war. Now I thought the reasons why we went to war might be very relevant to the drafting of the Declaration of Independence, but terms like "taxation without representation" and "The Stamp Act" did not immediately come to her mind. Yet, if I remember correctly, she was getting a "B" in her class.

This is why you have to be involved in your child's education and continue to ask her questions about what she is learning in order to evaluate her level of progress. You should start to do this early and get a real grip on the level of knowledge your child has in each important subject area.

One way to do this is to evaluate your child's performance on her homework. If, for instance, your child brings home math worksheets almost every night and she is able to complete most of the problems by getting the correct answers on her own, you may conclude that she is grasping most of what is required of her in this section of math. If, however, she is having trouble finding the correct answer to, say, nine out of the twenty problems she may have for homework, then you can conclude that she may be having trouble grasping much of the information she should be learning in this section of math. You can then work with her at home and/or bring this to the attention of the teacher and ask for additional guidance to address those problems with which she may be having difficulty.

At this stage you may still see most of your child's work, as many teachers will continue to send home tests to be signed and graded homework in "homework folders." So you can see exactly what your child is getting on homework papers, tests, and quizzes. (Many schools have begun to post everything online). Thus her grade should be no real surprise to you or to her. You will just want to make sure she is actually grasping the information she is being tested on and that she is being properly prepared for the next grade.

Thus, fourth grade can provide you with a real opportunity to set expectations around "letter grades" and your child's actual understanding of class work.

Let's take a deeper look into what mathematics might look like in the fourth grade.

Chapter 2

Fourth-Grade Math

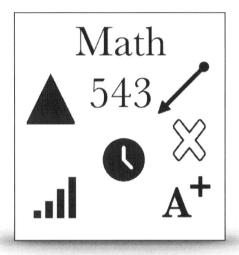

Your child probably got a good introduction to multiplication in third grade. The focus was more than likely on multiplication facts (0–9 or 0–12), so the first part of fourth grade will probably be spent on reinforcing these multiplication facts. You can support these efforts by having your child complete multiplication problems at home. It will be very important for your child to have a good handle on her multiplication facts. If she doesn't master them, moving on to some of the next steps in mathematics will be difficult.

Some time might also be spent on adding and subtracting three- and four-digit numbers, just to make sure your child has these skills fully developed. After all, adding and subtracting is something people do for the rest of their lives. So problems like 345 + 454 = 799 or 8,987 − 8,093 = 894 will probably be given to your child. She will not only be expected to solve problems like this, but any addition or subtraction problem involving "regrouping" or "carrying over" will also be expected.

So once your child has addition, subtraction, and basic multiplication "under her belt," she will be taught more advanced forms of multiplication. For instance, multiplying multi-digit numbers will be introduced. Problems like 45 x 8 or 98 x 39 or 345 x 7 will be explored. You can see if she knows her multiplication facts for basic problems like 9 x 9 or 7 x 5, then moving on to the more advanced forms of multi-digit multiplication won't be as difficult.

Your child will then be given more practical applications for multiplication in the form of word problems.

If Jane wants to buy three toys worth $3.50 each, four books worth $2.80 each, and five candles worth $5.00 each, how much money will she spend overall?

This problem will force your child to use what she has learned about addition and multiplication to solve a practical problem. You can see how mathematics here has a very real application, one which your child might have to apply in her everyday life. Other aspects of mathematics have very real applications, but sometimes those "real-world" applications may be unclear at first. We will try to explore these applications as we walk through the skills your child will be taught in school.

As we have alluded to, adding and subtracting monetary amounts will show up more and more in your child's homework. Here is a great opportunity to reinforce this skill in the work you do with your child at home. At this stage, have your child go with you and order or purchase items in a restaurant or store. Observe your child as she picks out the right amount of money to give the cashier and as she waits to receive the right amount of money in change. Help her as she goes through this process and determine if she can estimate how much money she should get back in change when she does these exercises.

As your child is solidifying these skills, the basics of division will also be taught. Just as she had to master multiplication facts for 0–9, she will also have to master division facts for 0–9. The same approach of repetition and practice at home that worked with multiplication will work with division. You can support your child's efforts by making up worksheets with basic division problems on them and having your child practice at home.

So, solving $81 \div 9 = 9$ or $28 \div 7 = 4$ will be something your fourth grader will be asked to do. Some teachers will introduce division of two- and three-digit numbers by a one-digit number. For example: $30 \div 6 = 5$, $270 \div 9 = 30$ or $488 \div 2 = 244$. So learning basic facts for division that correspond to the multiplication facts your fourth grader already knows will be key to her success in division.

Being able to find remainders in division problems will also be taught. Solving a problem like:

$960 \div 7 = 137$ with a remainder "R" of 1.

This type of long division may be the first time your child is really challenged to follow steps, in an ordered fashion, to come up with the correct answer. This may require some patience and a good deal of practice because...

First you have to find out how many times 7 goes into 9.

Since 7 goes into 9 one time, there will be 2 left over.

Bringing down the 6, now you have to determine how many times 7 will go into 26.

Since 7 goes into 26 three times, you now have 5 left over.

Bringing down the 0, you now have to determine how many times 7 goes into 50.

Since 7 goes into 50 seven times, you now have 1 left over.

There are no more numbers to bring down, so you are left with a remainder of 1.

$$
\begin{array}{r}
137 \text{ R}1 \\
7\overline{)960} \\
-\underline{7} \\
26 \\
-\underline{21} \\
50 \\
-\underline{49} \\
1
\end{array}
$$

Your answer is 137 with a remainder of 1.

Your child will have to divide, then multiply, then subtract for the hundreds place, the tens place, and the ones place in order to find the right answer. You can see how being able to follow steps, knowing multiplication facts, and being skilled at subtraction helps a child solve division problems.

Your child will continue to hear certain mathematical terminology when it comes to division, so let's take a moment to review some common terminology now.

Addition:

An Addend + An Addend = Sum

$5 + 6 = 11$

5 and 6 are Addends and 11 is the Sum

Subtraction:

The Minuend – The Subtrahend = Difference

$9 - 7 = 2$

9 is the Minuend, 7 is the Subtrahend, and 2 is the Difference

Multiplication:

A Factor x A Factor = Product

$4 \times 3 = 12$

4 is a Factor, 3 is a Factor, and 12 is the Product

Division:

A Dividend ÷ A Divisor = Quotient

$8 \div 4 = 2$

8 is the Dividend, 4 is the Divisor, and 2 is the Quotient

Multiplication is the opposite of division, so as your child learns division, he or she will also be asked to find the factors of certain numbers. For example, 6, 2, 12, 1, 3, and 4 are all factors of 12. Consequently, 12 can be divided by

6, 2, 3, 4, 12, and 1 evenly. Refreshing your memory with these terms can help you provide guidance to your child.

Another skill your child will be encouraged to develop is the ability to check answers mentally. For instance, addition and subtraction are inverse (opposite) operations, so you can use subtraction to evaluate the correctness of addition problems and vice versa.

78 + 9 = 87

Check: 87 − 9 = 78

---

98 − 67 = 31

Check: 67 + 31 = 98

Since multiplication and division are inverse operations, multiplication can be used to check division problems and division can be used to check multiplication problems.

18 ÷ 2 = 9

Check: 9 x 2 = 18

---

15 x 3 = 45

Check: 45 ÷ 3 = 15

You can remind your child about the use of these techniques to help her check her answers when needed.

Your child will also work more with fractions and decimals. As we alluded to earlier, children in the fourth grade will work with adding and subtracting monetary amounts. These monetary amounts are written in the form of decimals. So your child must understand that $5.89 means the 5 represents 5 one-dollar bills (or 500 pennies), 8 represents 8 dimes (or 80 pennies), and the 9 represents 9 pennies.

As your child works with other, non-monetary, numbers in decimal form, he or she will have to identify the place value for numbers before and after the decimal. For instance:

12.98

- 1 is in the tens place

- 2 is in the ones place

- 9 is in the tenths place

- 8 is in the hundredths place

If you were looking at this number as if it were a monetary amount, you would have:

- 1 ten-dollar bill

- 2 one-dollar bills

- 9 dimes (or 90 pennies)

- 8 pennies

A decimal point is used to simply separate whole numbers (those numbers to the left of the decimal point) from values less than one (those numbers to the right of the decimal point). The numbers to the left of the decimal point are both > or = one dollar (a ten-dollar bill and two one-dollar bills) and the numbers to the right of the decimal point are < one dollar (90 cents and 8 cents).

Your child may also learn to add and subtract fractions with like denominators, such as $1/4 + 2/4 = 3/4$ or $3/5 - 2/5 = 1/5$. These concepts can be easily reinforced at home: $1/4$ of a cake plus $2/4$ of a cake equals $3/4$ of a cake.

Being able to understand and order numbers up to one million may also be addressed in fourth grade. This wouldn't be a bad time to let your child know about the concept of infinity, if you haven't already done so. In reality we could keep counting forever and never stop because there is no limit to how high numbers go. Some children find that concept interesting and get excited when they know that after the millions, there are billions, then trillions, and so on. Children at this stage may not be introduced to negative numbers yet, but the same principle of infinity applies to negative numbers as well.

More work may be done with measurements using the U.S. Customary System of Measurement and the Metric

System. You can supplement these activities by exposing your child to common units of measurement at home.

Units of Measurement

1 inch **=** 2.54 centimeters

1 foot (or 12 inches) **=** 0.3048 meter

1 yard (or 36 inches) **=** 0.9144 meter

39.37 inches **=** 1 meter

1 mile (or 5,280 feet) **=** 1.6093 kilometers

See more in our chapter on Mathematical Activities.

In preparation for algebra, your child might be taught how to fill in missing numbers or operations in a given number sentence. For example 7 x ? = 49 or 3 ? 6 = 18. All of this helps to improve your child's mathematical skills in a way that will help him or her be well-rounded in this discipline. Let's now look at some skills you may wish to evaluate as they relate to your fourth grader.

Chapter 3

Fourth-Grade Mathematical Skills

You can help assess your child's development at home and help her as she learns new skills in the classroom. Some fundamental skills are listed below that, if built upon, will help your child in this grade and in later years.

MATHEMATICAL SKILLS:

$$
\begin{array}{r}
137 \text{ R}1 \\
7\overline{)960} \\
-7 \\
\hline
26 \\
-21 \\
\hline
50 \\
-49 \\
\hline
1
\end{array}
$$

1. My child is able to correctly solve three- and four-digit addition and subtraction problems, even those that require "regrouping" or "carrying over." For instance, 3,489 + 894 = 4,383 or 987 − 78 = 909.

2. My child knows, with proficiency, multiplication facts for 0–12. For example, 2 x 1 = 2, 2 x 2 =4 ... 12 x 1 = 12, 12 x 2 = 24, 12 x 3 = 36, etc.

3. My child is able to correctly solve multiplication problems involving multiple digits, such as 27 x 5 = 135 or 50 x 40 = 2,000.

4. My child can correctly use multiple operations to solve word problems. Bob buys four toy cars for $4 each and five toy trucks for $6 each. How much will he spend overall? (A child must first multiply 4 x $4 to get $16, then multiply 5 x $6 to get $30. The child must then add to get the final answer: 16 + 30 = $46).

5. My child is able to add and subtract monetary amounts with proficiency, such as $4.50 + $5.78 = $10.28.

6. My child knows division facts for 0–9 (e.g. $9 \div 3 = 3$ or $81 \div 9 = 9$) and can divide multiple-digit numbers by single-digit numbers (e.g. $360 \div 6 = 60$).

7. My child is able to mentally check his or her answers by employing the use of inverse operations when necessary.

   - Subtraction can be used to evaluate the correctness of an addition problem and addition can be used to check a subtraction problem.

   - Since multiplication and division are inverse operations, multiplication can be used to check division problems and division can be used to check multiplication problems.

8. My child understands place values for decimals to the hundredths place. For example: 12.98

   1 is in the tens place

   2 is in the ones place

   9 is in the tenths place

   8 is in the hundredths place

9. My child can add and subtract fractions with like denominators. For example, $1/3 + 1/3 = 2/3$.

10. My child has a good understanding of the basic units of the U.S. Customary System of Measurement and the Metric System (i.e., inches, centimeters, ounces, pounds, grams, liters, and gallons).

Chapter 4
Mathematical Activities

To help your child develop and progress in the use of these skills, consider doing the following activities, which can assist you in the work you do with your child at home. The activities are segmented into three of the principles we reviewed earlier: Educational Exposure At Home, Repetition and Practice, and Encouraged Articulation.

EDUCATIONAL EXPOSURE AT HOME

Real-Life Exposure:

As your child learns about multiplication, division, and more advanced addition and subtraction in school, seek opportunities to expose him or her to these things at home.

For example, as you budget your finances for the month have your child help you with certain items. Most children at this age probably have no idea what things cost, so this might be an eye-opening experience. Give your child an estimate of how much you spend in groceries each week and have him or her figure out how much money you will need for the entire month for groceries.

You can take one month's electricity bill and have your child figure out how much it will cost you in services for the entire year, if your monthly charges stayed about the same. You can do the same with your phone bill, cable bill, etc.

Plan a trip to the movies for your family. Have your fourth grader figure out how much money you will need for the entire family. If tickets cost $7.50 per person (I only think in terms of matinees), how much money will you need for tickets? If you purchase a large container of popcorn, which costs $8, and each person gets a medium drink at $5 per drink, how much money will you need for snacks? You can do the same exercise for a trip to a sporting event, a play, a museum, etc.

If your child is buying presents for a number of family members at one time, give her a certain amount of money and have her divide that amount by the number of family members for whom she wants to buy presents in order to figure out how much she can spend on each person.

As we have mentioned, continue to have your child actively figure out the correct change for items as you purchase things in a store. This may take some time because there will be people around, but be patient —"practice makes perfect."

The idea here is to find ways for your child to use addition, subtraction, multiplication, and division in your everyday lives. She will see that mathematics has real applications for her life and may even take more of an interest in it in school.

REPETITION AND PRACTICE

Multiplication and Division:

If you have been practicing drills with your child for multiplication, you should continue to do so. Have your child solve thirty multiplication problems in sixty seconds for facts from 0–12. Zero and one should be pretty easy because any number multiplied by "0" equals "0," and any number multiplied by "1" equals that number. For the rest of the facts, have your child complete problems ranging from 0–12. For example, focus on the "2s"…2 x 0, 2 x 1, 2 x 2, 2 x 3…2 x 12. Next focus on the "3s" and so on, until you complete the "12s." Create the worksheets yourself or use other resources like the Internet or workbooks you can purchase in stores.

Repetition and practice are also very important for division. Once your child has successfully completed thirty multiplication problems for the facts noted above, have your child do the same exercise for division facts from 0–9.

For example, $1 \div 1 = 1$; $2 \div 1 = 2$; $3 \div 1 = 3$ … $2 \div 2 = 1$; $4 \div 2 = 2$; $6 \div 2 = 3$, etc. up through $9 \div 9 = 1$; $18 \div 9 = 2$; $27 \div 9 = 3$, etc. Please note that division by "0" is not possible because you simply cannot divide a number by nothing.

Reinforcing Fractions:

As your child begins to learn about adding and subtracting fractions, give her additional problems at home that mirror problems in her homework. Simply take old homework assignments and see if your child is able to complete the same problems, again, as time goes by. This can be done just to make sure she understands the concept and is skilled at performing these tasks. (You can also use examples from her textbook for additional practice.)

Remembering Measurements:

Obtain a measuring cup or utensils at home. Under your supervision, have your child measure out liquids (or other items) needed for certain recipes—a cup of water, $\frac{1}{2}$ cup of milk, 2 oz. of margarine, etc.

Use common household items like rulers, measuring tapes, measuring cups, etc. to help you explain what these units mean.

For your reference, included are some common units of measurement within the U.S. Customary System and the Metric System.

U.S. Customary System

Length

---

1 foot = 12 inches

3 feet = 36 inches (or 1 yard)

1 mile = 5,280 feet

Measuring Liquids

---

8 fluid ounces = about 1 cup

16 fluid ounces = 1 pint (or about 2 cups)

32 fluid ounces = 1 quart (or about 4 cups)

128 fluid ounces = 1 gallon (or about 16 cups)

Measuring Solids

---

1 ounce = 0.0625 pound

16 ounces = 1 pound

1 ton = 2,000 pounds

Metric System

Length

---

1 millimeter (mm) **=** 0.001 meter

1 centimeter (cm) **=** 0.01 meter

1 decimeter (dm) **=** 0.1 meter

1 decameter (dkm) **=** 10 meters

1 hectometer (hm) **=** 100 meters

1 kilometer (km) **=** 1,000 meters

- Note that 1 meter is equal to 39.37 inches.

Volume

---

1 milliliter (ml) **=** 0.001 liter

1 centiliter (cl) **=** 0.01 liter

1 deciliter (dl) **=** 0.1 liter

1 dekaliter (dkl) **=** 10 liters

1 hectoliter (hl) **=** 100 liters

1 kiloliter (kl) **=** 1,000 liters

Mass

1 milligram (mg) = 0.001 gram

1 centigram (cg) = 0.01 gram

1 decigram (dg) = 0.1 gram

1 decagram (dkg) = 10 grams

1 hectogram (hg) = 100 grams

1 kilogram (kg) = 1000 grams

U.S. Customary System and Metric System Common Equivalents

1 inch = 2.54 centimeters

39.37 inches = 1 meter

1 mile (or 5,280 feet) = 1.6093 kilometers

1 quart (or 32 fluid ounces) = 0.9463 liter

1.056 quarts = 1 liter

1 pound (or 16 ounces) = 453.59 grams

2.2046 pounds = 1 kilogram (or 1,000 grams)

1 ton (or 2,000 pounds) = 907.18 kilograms

ENCOURAGED ARTICULATION

Articulation:

As we have discussed, when children get into higher grades, teachers will look for them to explain their answers. So you should continue to encourage your child to explain what she is thinking when it comes to solving math problems. Instead of only drilling your child or making her write out answers, you can mix things up from time to time by asking her to explain how she would solve a given problem. Your child might not be able to do this proficiently yet, but working through the process in her mind and verbally is good practice.

Neat and Legible:

Fourth grade math homework may require children to go through several steps and perform multiple operations to find the correct answer. As your child completes her math homework, check to see if she is showing all of her work, if she is writing her work in a neat and legible manner, and, obviously, if she is able to explain how she got her answer. This will become more and more important for problems requiring multiple steps because a teacher may want to see "how" a child got the answer and if the child understands all of the steps that must be followed.

Her work must also be neat and legible so that the teacher is able to follow it.

Mental Math:

Encourage your child to use mental math and inverse operations to check her answers. For instance if your child is unsure whether $72 \div 8 = 9$, ask her to multiply 9×8 and she should get 72.

Chapter 5

Reading and Writing in Fourth Grade

As mentioned in our earlier book on the third grade, not much time will be spent teaching the basics of reading in the fourth grade. Teachers will expect that most of the groundwork has already been laid, and their focus will shift to applying reading skills to various situations. It will be essential for your child to become more of an independent learner. Let's say, for example, your child is given an assignment to do in class. In second or third grade the teacher might have read all of the instructions to the class and made sure that the entire class understood them before starting the assignment. As your child progresses through fourth grade, her teacher may give out assignments in class and expect her to be able to follow the instructions on her own. She will have to have good comprehension skills in order to be able to decipher what the instructions are actually asking her to do.

In another circumstance, your child might be studying social studies in class. Her teacher may give her an assignment to find out information about the climate and resources of a specific region in the United States, say the Northeast. As the year progresses, the teacher might expect your child to be able to locate this information on her own in her social studies book. In earlier grades a teacher might have had the entire class turn to the right page in the book and read the information together. In fourth grade, the teacher may expect every child to be able to look up the information in the table of contents or in the index, find the correct pages to go to, and take notes on the required information based on the instructions. The teacher might also expect your child to be able to look up words in a glossary related to this topic or to interpret a chart on the given information in order to answer questions.

This is an example of how the skills your child learned in earlier grades (how to find information in a table of contents, in an index, etc.) may be used in subsequent grades.

Even though a child may have been taught much of the basics of reading in earlier grades, there are still many skills to sharpen. Your child should continue to practice reading on a regular basis. When she comes across words she doesn't know, she should use her ability to sound out words to try to come up with the correct pronunciation. She should look at the manner in which a word is used in a sentence to try to figure out its meaning. Finally, she should be able to look up most words in a dictionary to try to find their meaning.

For example, if a passage read:

"John was a 'straight-A' student. He never got bad grades on his report card, so getting a "D" in English was an aberration for him."

If your child is unfamiliar with the word "aberration," she should be able to employ some techniques that may help her figure out how to pronounce the word. For instance, she could break the word apart by syllables: ab-er-ra-tion. She could also look at the other clues in the passage to help her figure out its meaning. If John was a "straight-A" student and never got bad grades, then "aberration" must mean something that's out of the normal or that doesn't usually happen. These are the kinds of skills your fourth grader should be refining.

This will take lots of practice. That is why you can't allow your child to stop reading outside of class simply because she has already learned how to read or because the teacher hasn't given specific reading assignments. Reading on her own will teach her so many skills and give her the necessary opportunities to refine the skills she has already developed.

As in earlier grades, your child will be asked to identify the main topic in many of the short stories and other types of material she reads. The only difference here is that the material she will be reading will be on a higher level and the topics will be more advanced. So reading really becomes a means by which your child can learn new and more in-depth information.

When it comes to writing, your child will be expected to expand upon the basic skills that were taught in third grade. For example, your child may now be expected to write about a topic using multiple paragraphs instead of just one paragraph. If you remember our formula for writing a good paragraph in third grade…

Topic Sentence

+ 2 or 3 **Supporting Sentences**

+ **Concluding Sentence**

= A Good Paragraph

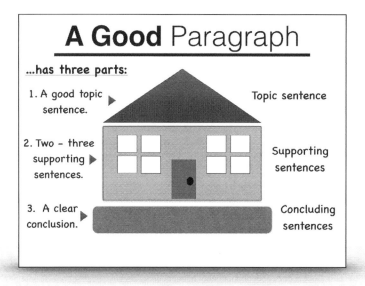

Well, we are going to expand on this formula just a bit. The basic premise will remain the same, except it will now be applied to multiple paragraphs. The formula now looks like this:

An Introductory Paragraph that Clearly States the Topic of the Report and has at least Two Main Ideas that Support the Topic

+

Two Paragraphs that Express Each Main Idea, with Details and Good Descriptive Words

+

A Concluding Paragraph That Sums Up the Main Ideas of the Report

= A Good Report

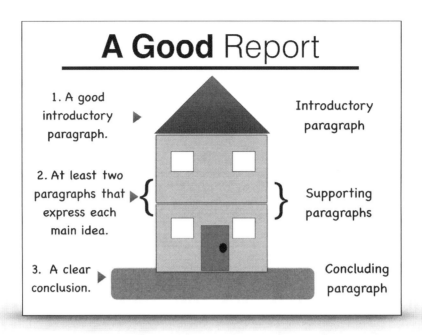

A Good Report

1. A good introductory paragraph. ▶ Introductory paragraph

2. At least two paragraphs that express each main idea. ▶ { } Supporting paragraphs

3. A clear conclusion. ▶ Concluding paragraph

So, in fourth grade:

- Your child may now have to write an introductory paragraph that clearly states the topic of the writing assignment or report.

- Your child may have to express two or three main ideas that support the topic.

- Your child will be asked to support these main ideas with details and examples.

- Your child will be asked to use transition words within or between each paragraph.

- Your child may also be asked to use many descriptive words and compelling verbs in his or her writing.

- Few mistakes in punctuation and grammar will be expected.

- Your child will be expected to stay on the topic throughout the entire paper.

- Finally, your child may be expected to correct her own work, to some degree. She may be asked to edit her writing and check for errors and omissions before turning in her work in class. Self-editing is an important part of writing.

The various forms of writing your child might be required to do are: imaginative and personal narratives (telling a story about a real or "imagined" personal experience), responses to a literary work, summaries of books and other kinds of reading material, or research reports. The same premise of having an introductory paragraph, main ideas to support the topic, details and examples, descriptive words, and a conclusion applies to all of these forms of writing.

This may sound like a significant jump, but it will likely be done over time and is not as complicated as it may seem. Many times teachers will give explicit instructions about what the composition should include and require each child to complete a rough draft (or "sloppy copy") before submitting the final copy. This gives the teacher an opportunity to give the child guidance and to identify areas in which the child needs to improve before the final assignment is submitted.

For example, let's say your child had to write an imaginative narrative entitled, "My Trip to the Moon." After turning in and receiving feedback on a rough draft, the final copy of this narrative writing might look like this:

My Trip to the Moon

"I went on a trip to the moon with my family and friends. My mom, dad, and my little sister all came on the trip. My best friends John and Diane also came along. The trip was exciting because we got to see a lot of cool things. It was also a scary trip because there were creepy aliens on the moon.

We went to the moon on a rocket. It was the fastest rocket in the world. We got to the moon in one minute. That was cool! The other exciting part of the trip happened when we got there. When we got off of the rocket we saw purple trees and green lights everywhere. It was just like a giant party. There was candy and food everywhere for everybody to eat. We walked around and stuffed our pockets with candy!

That's when we saw the scary aliens. They had big ears and long orange claws. They came after us with their sharp teeth and we all ran back to the rocket. We made it to the rocket just in time.

We flew back to earth in just one minute. We all said the trip was amazing. This is how my trip to the moon was exciting and scary at the same time."

The topic of this narrative is "My Trip to the Moon." The two main ideas expressed in this story are that the trip was "exciting" and "scary." The writer stated the topic and the two main ideas in the introductory paragraph.

The two main ideas were supported by details and examples. The trip was exciting because they traveled on the "fastest rocket in the world" and the moon was just like "one giant party, with candy and food everywhere." The trip was scary because "there were creepy aliens" who came after them "with sharp teeth."

The narrative also had many descriptive words that helped the reader picture what was going on—"purple trees, green lights, long orange claws, and sharp teeth."

Finally, the writer stayed on the topic of "My Trip to the Moon" throughout the story. These are the kinds of things you can look for as you help your child with fourth grade writing assignments. You should also look for any misspelled words, mistakes in grammar or punctuation, and make sure each paragraph is indented and starts with a capital letter.

Your child's teacher may send home a writing guide that may give clues about what to look for in your child's writing. If your teacher does not automatically send something home, ask for one. Most states, school districts, or schools have guides for what an effective writing sample should look like. You can also go online to see examples of guides as many states and school districts provide examples in preparation for standardized tests. If you do not have access to a checklist or guide, use the following to help you assist your child in evaluating writing assignments.

Writing Checklist:

Do I have an introductory paragraph that clearly states the topic of the paper and two or three main ideas that support the topic?

Do I have a separate paragraph to explain each main idea?

Do I have details in each paragraph that support the main ideas?

Do I use adjectives to describe the people, places, and things in each paragraph?

Do I use words that describe how I feel or what I think?

Do I have a concluding paragraph that sums up the main ideas of my report?

Other Items:

Are the paragraphs indented?

Do the paragraphs have the correct punctuation and spelling?

Encourage your child to read over the paragraphs to check for any corrections that may be needed before giving it to you to read. Self-editing is an important part of writing.

In the case of a research report, your child will be asked to go to more than one source for information before completing her assignment. It is important for her to know that information comes in many forms and that the best way to research a topic is to go to multiple sources before writing a report. Your child will be taught that it is necessary to cite her sources when doing a research report so that the reader can know where she got her information and possibly read those sources as well.

Facts are also important in a research project. If your child is writing a report on Martin Luther King Jr., facts such as when and where he was born, where he went to school, who he married, famous speeches he made, etc. are all important pieces of information to include. You can help your child by making sure she asks herself different questions before she starts reading as a part of a research assignment. If your child knows what information she may want to include in her report before she starts reading (date of birth, famous speeches, etc.), it will be much easier for her to take note of that information or highlight it when she comes across it in her reading.

Taking notes and highlighting important information is a skill your fourth grader will need to develop. It will become more critical to her success as she begins to take more notes in class, studies more from assigned reading material, and completes more research projects as she gets older.

When it comes to grammar, your fourth grader may learn more about the Parts of Speech. For example:

Regular Verbs – Verbs are words that show action or a state of being. "I walk to school everyday." "Walk" shows the action in this sentence. When regular verbs are written in the past tense an "ed" is typically added: walk/walked, call/called, live/lived, etc.

Irregular Verbs – These are verbs that change, sometimes completely, when written in the past tense, such as go/went, sleep/slept, do/did, etc. For example, "be" is an irregular verb. Its past tense forms are "was" and "were." Its present tense forms are "be," "am," "is," and "are."

Adjectives – These are words that modify a noun by describing it. "The long road was dark and dirty." "Long," "dark," and "dirty" are all adjectives that describe the noun "road."

Adverbs – These are words that describe verbs, adjectives, or other adverbs. "The girl ran quickly." "Ran" is the verb in this sentence and "quickly," describes how the girl ran.

Prepositions – These words show how a noun or pronoun is related to other words in a sentence. "The jar is in the backpack with the other material." "In" shows where the jar is and "with" shows where the jar is in relation to the "other material." "About," "in," "with," "from," "to," "above," "on," and "underneath" are all prepositions.

Conjunctions – These are words that join other words, clauses, and phrases together. For example, "and" is a conjunction. "She is a track star and an athlete." The words "but" and "or" are also conjunctions.

Your child was more than likely introduced to nouns, pronouns, adjectives, and verbs in earlier grades. Thus, your child will be expected to effectively use many or all of these parts of speech in her writing as she learns more and more about them in school.

Another skill that may be taught is how to identify a simple subject and a simple predicate in a sentence. A subject is the person or thing that performs the action in a sentence. A predicate is the part of a sentence that contains the verb or action and says something about the subject.

The boy ran down the street.

"The boy" is the subject of this sentence and "ran down the street" is the predicate.

Lastly, by the end of the fourth grade your child should be able to write neatly and fluently in both print and cursive. Some practice might be done with cursive early in the fourth-grade year, since students learned cursive for the first time most likely in the third grade. Your child's teacher might make comments and suggestions about your child's writing to make sure she is forming her letters correctly.

One of the areas of opportunity I had to work on with my son was helping him to have neat handwriting in math and on writing assignments. I had to explain to him that even if he put the right answer down on his paper, if no one could read it, it would still be marked wrong by the teacher. The teacher can only be expected to guess what you mean if your writing is not clear. You can reinforce neat handwriting by having your child practice this skill at home. Remember, your work is never "right" if no one can read it!

Chapter 6

Fourth-Grade Reading and Writing Skills

You can help assess your child's development at home and help him as he learns new skills in the classroom. Some fundamental skills are listed below that, if built upon, will help your child in this and later grades.

READING AND WRITING SKILLS:

Reading Log

Author	Title	Date Completed
1. _____	_____	_____
2. _____	_____	_____
3. _____	_____	_____

Use a simple **READING LOG** to help **SHARPEN** your child's reading skills.

Reading a **VARIETY** of books can **INCREASE** comprehension & vocabulary.

★ **CELEBRATE** when your child **READS** ten books!

1. My child is able to read a book on a fourth grade level, explain its main idea, and give specific details about what happened in the book. (The reading level for many children's books is printed right on the back of the book near the bottom).

2. My child reads chapter books outside of required assignments for school on a regular basis—about two per month. (The books can be about one hundred or more pages in length.)

3. My child is able to read assigned material in textbooks and pick out the main information communicated in the material.

4. My child is able to locate information in his or her textbook (or any other book) by using the table of contents, the index, the glossary, chapter titles, and sub-titles, etc.

5. My child is able to use reading strategies and techniques to try to figure out the meanings and pronunciations of unfamiliar words.

6. My child is able to read instructions for homework, primarily on his or her own, with understanding and clarity. (Sometimes you may have to help your child understand the instructions, but for the most part your child should be able to figure out what they are asking him or her to do.)

7. My child is able to write a composition consisting of multiple paragraphs that have the following:

    An Introductory Paragraph that Clearly States the Topic of the Report and has at least Two Main Ideas that Support the Topic

    +

    Two Paragraphs that Express **Each Main Idea**, with Details and Good Descriptive Words

    +

    A Concluding Paragraph That Sums Up the Main Ideas of the Report

8. My child is able to write an effective multi-paragraph composition describing a personal experience. My child can do the same for an imaginative story or research report.

9. My child understands what nouns, pronouns, verbs, adverbs, adjectives, and conjunctions are and can use them in his or her writing.

10. My child is able to write fluently and legibly in cursive and in print.

Chapter 7

Reading and Writing Activities

The following activities can aid in the work you do with your child at home. As with earlier activities, these activities are segmented into three of the principles we reviewed earlier: Educational Exposure At Home, Repetition and Practice, and Encouraged Articulation.

EDUCATIONAL EXPOSURE AT HOME

Fourth grade is a great time to expose your child to new educational concepts and ideas. This is a great stage where your child can read and make sense of a lot of things around him or her while still being a "kid" who can be excited about discovering new information.

By now, you may be able to observe some of the things your child has an interest in—music, science, math, sports, art, computers, etc. Expand upon your child's interest by encouraging him or her to read more about the topic of this interest.

See if you can find examples of famous people who have excelled in the field in which your child is interested. Look up these famous people on the Internet or in books or in magazines. What did they do to excel in this field? What was their life like growing up? Can your child accomplish the same thing this famous person did?

Also, expose your child to subjects she may not be interested in or about which she does not have a lot of knowledge.

For example, read a book or go online to discover how the human body works. How is blood pumped throughout the body? How do we breathe? How does the brain and the nervous system work?

Find out how airplanes are able to fly. What keeps them from falling to the ground? After you find out the answer, have a paper airplane contest with your child. See whose airplane can fly the farthest. What was it about the airplane that flew the farthest that allowed it to win?

There are plenty of websites or television programs that explain how things work. On television networks dedicated to science, and some of those dedicated to children, there are programs that go behind the scenes to show how things work and how they are made. Spend a specified amount of time with your child viewing information that is educational.

Take time to expose your child to geography.

Take a map and circle all of the places you and your child have been. Talk about the areas or regions of the country in which those places are located. What are the differences between some of the places you have visited and where you actually live? What cities and/or states would you and your child like to visit?

Learn more about the state in which you live. What kinds of products are made in your state? What is the capital? How many people live in your state? In your city? Who is the governor of your state? What are some special facts about your state?

Pick a professional sport—football, basketball, baseball, or hockey. Get a map and circle all of the cities that have a professional team. This is a great way to use sports as an opportunity to teach your child something educational. Your child can learn a little about geography and how sports teams are segmented into different divisions. How many cities have a professional football team? Baseball team? Basketball team? How many states have more than one professional team? Why? Which city has two football teams, two baseball teams, and at least one basketball team that all carry its name? Why do you think this is so?

REPETITION AND PRACTICE

The number one thing you can do to enhance your child's educational outlook is to have him or her read on a regular basis. Now may be a good time to start keeping a log of the books your child reads.

By now the books your child reads should be about one hundred pages long, at least, and be on a fourth-grade reading level.

Take note of each book your child completes. Give him special recognition when he finishes his first hundred-page book. Try to pace his efforts to about two books per month, if possible. That may mean thirty minutes or so a night reading or more time spent on weekends reading instead of doing other activities like watching television. If your child is able to read twenty to twenty-four books a year, on various subjects in different genres, your child should be well on his way to expanding his knowledge overall. Keeping a log simply lets you track his progress and gives him a way to reflect on his accomplishments.

Reading Log

Author	Title	Date Completed
1. _____	_____	_____
2. _____	_____	_____
3. _____	_____	_____

Use a simple **READING LOG** to help **SHARPEN** your child's reading skills.

Reading a **VARIETY** of books can **INCREASE** comprehension & vocabulary.

★ **CELEBRATE** when your child **READS** ten books!

After and during each book your child reads, stop and ask him or her questions about the book.

Who are the main characters? What is the main problem in the book or what is the plot? If you were the main character in this book, what would you do? How do you think this book will end? If you could change something about this book what would it be? If you had to write a book on the same topic, what would you write?

From time to time, ask your child to write three or four paragraphs at home about various topics. This is a good way to see how well your child is really developing his or her writing skills. Look for things like a clearly stated topic, main ideas to support the topic, details and examples supporting the main ideas, descriptive words, a good conclusion, and good use of grammar.

Topics that you can use may be: "My First Day at School," "The Perfect Birthday Party," "My Favorite Thing to Do," "If Dogs Could Fly," "The Best Book I Ever Read," "My Favorite Toy of All Time," "My Day at the Amusement Park," "How to Teach Your Mom and Dad to Play Video Games," etc. You can make up your own topics…try to make them fun, get your child to use her imagination, and use these writing activities to evaluate how well she is developing her writing skills.

Encourage your child to edit his or her work by using a writing checklist. You can use the following as a guide.

Writing Checklist

Do I have an introductory paragraph that clearly states the topic of the paper and two or three main ideas that support the topic?

Do I have a separate paragraph to explain each main idea?

Do I have details in the each paragraph that support the main ideas?

Do I use adjectives to describe the people, places, and things in each paragraph?

Do I use words that describe how I feel or what I think?

Do I have a concluding paragraph that sums up the main ideas of my report?

Other Items:

Are the paragraphs indented?

Do the paragraphs have the correct punctuation and spelling?

Encourage your child to read over her paragraphs to check for any corrections that may be needed before giving it to you to read. Self-editing is an important part of writing.

Sit down with your child and review what nouns, pronouns, verbs, adverbs, adjectives, conjunctions, subjects, and predicates are. See if your child can give you an example of each and explain back to you what they are. Your child's explanation doesn't have to be a "fancy" explanation, it just has to be clear to you that he or she knows what these things are and can use them if needed in a sentence.

ENCOURAGED ARTICULATION

As your child completes her homework each night, from time to time ask her to explain to you exactly what she has to do. This should give you an indication of whether or not she is reading the instructions and understands what she needs to do. This is a very important issue because you may be surprised to find out how many children in later grades have difficulty explaining what a teacher has asked them to do. This will be even more important in high school when children are given more complex assignments and are expected to be able to follow the assignment's instructions.

If your child has a major project to do, sit down with him or her and review the instructions. As mentioned above, this is a skill that will have to be developed.

Take the time to review chapters and reading assignments in your child's textbooks. Have your child explain to you the major points of a chapter. See if he or she can pick out important words or concepts as well as find information in the glossary or by using the index.

Chapter 8

Parent/Teacher Conferences

You can use these pages to take notes during your conference or simply reference them as you make a list of the items you'd like to discuss with your child's teacher.

Interaction #1: "Back to School Night" (Beginning of the School Year)

The questions below can typically be answered at the traditional "Back to School Night." You can use the following pages to take notes as needed. If you are unable to attend, make sure you get this information from your child's teacher.

Questions

1. How will homework, class projects and tests be communicated to children and parents?

2. How do you typically like to receive communications from parents; via email, phone or written notes (write email address or phone number below)?

3. Will there be any other assessments done of my child's skills and will I see the results?

4. Are there any major projects that will be done during this marking period?

5. How are grades determined? What does my child have to do to get an "A" (or its equivalent "Skilled) in each of the subjects taught?

6. By the end of the year, what do you expect my child to be able to do in math, reading and writing?

7. Additional questions or comments (e.g., Specific things I want to mention or things my child wants me to say. Is there anything else I need to know? Etc...)

Interaction # 2: Live Conference

Many schools will schedule conferences early in the second marking period. This will provide you with an opportunity to discuss your child's progress in key areas.

Questions

1. What are my child's strengths when it comes to reading, writing and math?

2. What are the areas for improvement for my child when it comes to reading, writing and math?

3. What specific activities can I do with my child at home to reinforce his strengths and to help him with his areas of improvement?

4. In which subjects does my child show the most (and least) interest in class?

5. By the middle of the year, what do you expect my child to be able to do in reading, writing and math?

6. Additional questions or comments (e.g., Specific things I want to mention or things my child wants me to say. Is there anything else I need to know? Etc...)

Interaction #3: Follow-up Discussion

Sometime after your first meeting your child's school may offer optional parent/teacher conferences, which provide an additional opportunity for you to check on your child's progress.

Questions

1. Have you seen improvements in the areas for growth we discussed earlier in the year?

2. Once again, what are areas of strengths you have observed relative to my child's skills?

3. What is being done in class to prepare my child to take the state's standardized exam (if applicable)?

4. What can I do, at home, to help prepare my child for success on the standardized exam?

5. By the end of the year, what do you expect my child to be able to do in reading, writing and math?

6. Additional questions or comments (e.g., Specific things I want to mention or things my child wants me to say. Is there anything else I need to know? Etc...)

Interaction #4: End of the School Year

If you are able to get just a few minutes with your child's teacher (or simply communicate via email) before the end of the school year, to find out what things you can expect for the next year, it may be well worth the effort.

Questions

1. Is my child ready for the next grade?

2. What will my child be expected to do in the next grade relative to reading, writing and math?

3. What activities can I do with my child, during the summer, to reinforce his strengths, enhance his areas for improvement and prepare him for the next grade? What resources do you recommend?

Additional notes:

Chapter 9

Education Success Stories: Thurgood Marshall

Front View of the Supreme Court - "Equal Justice Under Law."

Thurgood Marshall was born on July 2nd in Baltimore, Maryland in 1908. His father was a porter or waiter for a railroad company and his mother was an elementary school teacher. They were very involved in teaching their children and, reportedly, Thurgood's father would take him down to the courthouse in Baltimore just to view court proceedings. His mother, being a schoolteacher, oversaw her children's development and made sure they got good educational foundations in school.

When Thurgood was a child, he would often "cut up" in school and for his punishment the school's principal made him read the Constitution.

When he got old enough, he went to college. He attended Lincoln University in Pennsylvania. (Note: Thurgood Marshall attended Lincoln University when Langston Hughes was there—Langston Hughes graduated in 1929 and Marshall graduated in 1930).

Thurgood Marshall graduated from Lincoln University, with honors, and he hoped to attend the University of Maryland's School of Law. The school did not accept black students and Thurgood made the choice to go to Howard University instead. This choice would prove to be a life-changing decision.

At Howard University he met Charles Hamilton Houston who was the dean of the school and a man who was determined to get enough cases through the judicial system in order to overthrow the "separate but equal" doctrine that persisted in the nation's school systems (and in many other areas of society). Houston took Marshall under his wing as one of his most outstanding students and became his mentor.

The two, along with many others, worked on studying the Constitution and devised an approach to challenge segregation via the courts.

They believed that separate facilities were not equal and they would set out on a journey across the South to prove it. When Thurgood Marshall graduated from Howard (he graduated at the top of his class), he opened up a law firm in Baltimore.

He and Charles Houston won a major case in the fight against segregation in 1936. In the *Murray v. Pearson* case Donald Murray was an African-American man who sought admission into the University of Maryland School of Law.

He was denied admission because of his race. In fact, no African-American student had been admitted to Maryland's law school since an 1890 student-led protest was launched against their being admitted. The judge ruled in Donald Murray's favor and Marshall and Houston had their first major win. Thurgood Marshall later became the Director-Counsel of the National Association for the Advancement of Colored People's (NAACP) Legal Defense and Education Fund.

He began to tirelessly fight against segregation and used the strategies given to him by Houston to coordinate hundreds of cases to challenge the "separate but equal" doctrine. It would be 21 years, from the time of Marshall's graduation from Howard University to the *Brown v. Board of Education* ruling by the Supreme Court. During that time

Marshall travelled extensively throughout the country building cases against segregation.

In his lifetime, he argued 32 cases before the Supreme Court and won 29 of them. He was the lead attorney, as you know, in the *Brown v. Board of Education* case which ended segregation in public schools and opened the way for the "separate but equal" doctrine to be challenged in other ways.

Note: Charles Hamilton Houston never got to see the end results of his fight against segregation because he died on April 22, 1950. The decision in the *Brown v. Board of Education* case was handed down on May 17, 1954.

Thurgood Marshall, however, continued to fight for equal rights through the courts. In 1961, he was appointed to the U.S. Court of Appeals, 2nd Circuit. There he issued over 100 rulings, which were all later upheld by the Supreme Court.

In 1965 he was appointed U.S. Solicitor General and won 74% of the cases he argued for the government.

He was appointed Associate Justice of the Supreme Court in 1967 and served in that position for 24 years, until his retirement on October 1, 1991.

Thurgood Marshall

July 2, 1908 - January 24, 1993

References:

Architect of the Capitol. Thurgood Marshall Federal Judiciary Building. Accessed July 2016. http://www.aoc.gov/capitol-buildings/thurgood-marshall-federal-judiciary-building

Friedman, Michael Jay, Neely, Mildred and Dudziak, Mary. U.S. Department of State. Bureau of International Information Programs. Justice for All: The Legacy of Thurgood Marshall. Accessed July 2016. http://photos.state.gov/libraries/amgov/30145/publications-english/thurgood_marshall.pdf

NAACP Legal Defense and Education Fund, History: Thurgood Marshall. Accessed July 2016. http://www.naacpldf.org/thurgood-marshall

Supreme Court of the United States. Members of the Supreme Court of the United States. Members in the Timeline. Accessed July 2016. http://www.supremecourt.gov/about/members.aspx

University of Maryland School of Law. Thurgood Marshall Law Library. Donald Gaines Murray and the Integration of the University of Maryland School of Law. Accessed July 2016.

Other references:

Educational Standards, Education World U.S. http://www.education-world.com/standards/national/index.shtml

National Council of Teachers of English. http://www.ncte.org/about/over/standards

National Council of Teachers of Mathematics. http://www.nctm.org/

Online Oregon Standards Newspaper, Oregon Department of Education. http://www.ode.state.or.us/teachlearn/real/newspaper/default.aspx

Made in the USA
Middletown, DE
11 August 2016